THE MISHAPS OF A
HOPELESS ROMANTIC

the mishaps of a hopeless romantic

FRANCESCA JOANNA

Francesca Joanna Martin

for those who love hopelessly.

author's note

welcome to my second collection of poetry.

i can't thank you enough for taking the time out of your day to read these poems of mine.

poetry has been the most alleviating escape for me. day-to-day, i experience new memories, events, and chapters that i'm always willing and inspired to write about. and i'm pretty sure that poetry has become a special part of me. ever since i published my first collection of poetry, *teenage melancholy*, i began writing this one. and that's when i knew that i've developed a new profound passion of writing.

life can sure be a way to piece different segments of stories together. and this is my way of doing so – writing poems. i'll never run out of things to say or write about, as i'm constantly journeying through this tough, fun, bittersweet, difficult, and messy ride of life.

therefore, this is the second book of poems i wrote while recollecting various chapters and stories of my life that i once encountered, including young love and heartache. and it may not be the end for some of these stories (i may experience them once again in the future, who knows), but it's always worth it to write them down to look back on and see how far you've come and grown from your earliest encounters with them. this applies to both the heart-wrenching and "being on cloud nine" type of stories.

and i hope you too can find a sense of solidarity, empathy, inspiration, and awareness, as that's all i want for you, the reader, to gain from reading these poems.

enjoy.

- francesca joanna

the definition of a ***hopeless romantic*** (n.)
(in my own words and in terms of this book.)

a person who searches for an idealistic love they so willingly believe exists, especially despite the shitty experiences they've dealt with from past relationships.

even though they've probably already gone through the ups and downs of love, they still hold this special hope that someday and sometime, they'll finally have their happy ending with that someone.

note: but even when they think they've found it, they experience the mishaps they've once felt without it – loneliness, loss, suffering, misery, pain, and most of all, heartbreak – once the person leaves them. and to make matters even worse, they gave the one they thought would be their all, their all.

but don't worry: you're not alone;
i'm a fellow hopeless romantic.
i've dealt with the same things you've dealt with too.
searching, longing, and romanticizing,
and i know it can hurt at times.

so i wrote this book just for you.

i can only hope that you find your peace
and realize that **self-love and self-care**
is the very first step in finding the love you truly deserve
and have been waiting for while reading this.
everything will be okay and i promise,
everything will be better once you realize this.
it's the healing process.

so take care; *i'm in this with you too.*

**you are on the path to realizations
and finding your true obligations.**

chapters

| 1 |

solitude

the state of being alone, with no one to have or to hold.

my brothers and cousins
make me feel ashamed
for bringing nobody
and being empty-handed
at family reunions.

- how my holidays are spent

although it's not real life,
i envy the characters in the movies
who happily end up together
after emotional roller coasters,
long distances from los angeles to new york city,
and drunken nights with bottles of wine.

- desires

they say you'd find
the right one at the right time.

question is,
when is it?

- right person, right time

my bedroom walls probably laugh at me
because they witness
the disappointed face i make
while lying on my bed
for the lack of my love life.

- *laughing stock*

you'd rather be someplace else
than right here.

and that's what breaks me
into these shattered pieces.

- shattered pieces

it's been 92 days and i still can't get over you. i don't know what to do, but i'm still wishing you'd come through.

- 92

experiencing long-term loneliness
should be considered
a *severe disease.*

- lonesome

who would've thought
missing a special someone
would be equivalent to
a dagger through the chest?

- resemblances

i'm in the cinema alone
with no hand
to hold.

- *solitude*

how much
does a perfect soulmate
cost these days?

- *PDA*

maybe your departure
wasn't the ending i wanted
but it's still the one

i unfortunately got.

- *i wish you stayed*

i wish we were together,
and it pains me to know
that we'll never be.

- the most realistic fact

the one i want
sees me as
the one to not want.

it's as simple as that.

- foolish crush

i'm not afraid to love;

i'm afraid of not being loved
the way i do.

- *unreciprocated*

i feel like
i will always just be
another girl to you.

not one
you would ever date,

and not one
you would ever *love*.

- useless

i hope that one day
you'll sit and realize
that maybe just maybe
you have feelings for me *too*.

- wishful thinking

we're all guilty of
admiring and adoring
someone we just can't have
at least once in our lives.

we just hate to admit it.

- we've all done it before

these seasons make me feel
lonelier each time.

winter because
i can never go ice skating in downtown
with another.

spring because
i can never go to the sunflower fields
with another.

summer because
i can never go to that amusement park
with another.

fall because
i can never go boat pedaling at the lake
with another.

these perfect ideas in my head
but no one to fulfill them with.

- a year in a wrap-up

do we need love
in order for us to survive?

no.

do we need love
in order for us to feel alright?

yes.

- *essential*

one time, i really liked this boy. but i was so afraid to let him know, so i went ahead and gave another the chance to do it for themselves.

time has passed, and it pains me because i wasn't the one to show him the world. i willingly let that ship sail away; and now someone else is steering that wheel and has him enjoying the ride instead.

- the world

i've grown so curious.

i just want to know
the exact date
i will meet my soulmate.

and it doesn't matter if it will take slow,
i just want to find my romeo.

- *searching*

i just want you here with me
when i am feeling scared and crumbling apart.

i just want you here with me
when i am feeling lost and don't know where to start.

i just want you here with me
when i am feeling empty and *need* you in my heart.

- please come home

i take back all that i said when you were on the verge of leaving and i did nothing to stop you, but only say okay. i wish you would've known that i never meant it, it was only the anger in me speaking. because now i'm all alone, i can't find home, and i just want to give you a call on the phone. but it's too late and things will never go back to the old ways let alone be the same.

- i fucked up

maybe i hoped and asked
for too much

that love became
unattainable.

- *expensive*

i'm in new york city;

the place i imagined
we could've spent
our anniversary.

- the city of dreams

what exactly
does moving on
from something unattainable
look like?

- i should just give up on love at this point

in the end,
i've only learned
how to see the world
in two different ways.

the made-up world,
where you and i
are together in the ways
i've pictured in my head.

and then there's
there's the actual world,
where you and i
are nothing but
perfect strangers.

- fantasy vs. reality

i know that i don't really need love or a relationship in order to stay healthy, live my life, or be successful. but why does it fucking feel like that nearly all the damn time?

i'm continuously and optimistically dwelling on the thought of love, and this is what happens when you're a *hopeless romantic.*

- the mishaps of a hopeless romantic

summer

my favorite season
without my favorite person.

so sad.

- july

i don't think i'm sad
because of the lack of a significant other.

i think it's because
i can never find him no matter the wait
or long-lasting patience i've spent.

and i'm seriously getting tired of it.

- *what does the word patience really mean?*

i just want to write
the most uplifting romantic poem
but i just can't
because i need the
real life point of view
in order to do so.

- *authenticity*

it doesn't matter if
he'll only be here for a while
and his love is not permanent.

i just want to quit
this heartbreak lifestyle
and that alone would feel so fortunate.

- tired of the loneliness and longing

i wish you'd see me
the same way
i see you.

i wish you'd think about me
the same way
i think about you.

but i'm wishing
for silly things.

- unattainable

i don't even want to be
patient anymore.

i just want someone
to love me
the ways i do with them.

- desperate needs

| 2 |

persistence

having the tendency to continue doing something, especially wrong, despite knowing what isn't good for you.

she was so desperate that
she didn't even dare
to take precaution on
the potential dangers
he could cause her.

- *reckless*

i've been told to stay away
from a person like you

but i went ahead and disobeyed
because it was us i wished to pursue.

- chasing

he didn't want you.

why is this fact
so damn hard to accept?

- refusal

don't you ever just want a person, yet you already know that they aren't good or right for you?

and you're still sitting there, thinking about them 24/7 and the idea that maybe just maybe they may feel the same fucking way about you.

but again, you need to accept the most difficult part and remind yourself about the reasons why they just aren't the one for you and that you'll eventually find better.

but you don't want to nor fucking can't.

- we can never work out.

i think i'm finally getting over you.

i say this, but damn well i don't mean it.

- favorite lie

funny thing is,
i'm still hoping
you'd show up
at my front door
wanting to try again

but you still never have
after all this time.

- long gone

it's so unfair
how you'd never dare
to let go of the one
you absolutely love

yet they're the same ones
who'd let you fall and slip away
without a single doubt.

- the one that got away

money comes and goes.

the same thing applies to love.

- the cycle

i've gone insane to the point where
if you were to come back,
you wouldn't even need to apologize.

i'll just welcome you back
with open arms.

- that's how much i still care about you

we fell off last year,
but for some odd reason,
i have this gut feeling that

you'll come back
sometime in the future
and we'll forget our damaged past.

and it doesn't matter
if this will take
months or years.

i just want you back.

- lost and found

i know i shouldn't feel this way for you,
but it's so damn hard
to avoid.

- ignoring the signs

even your wrongdoings,
repetitive or not,

didn't stop me
from running back
to you.

oh god,
i feel like
a fucking fool.

- a lesson never learned

i've been broken
so many times already.

why do i still even have
a little faith and leniency in me?

- it's like i don't even care

i'm holding onto love

like

i'm holding on for dear life.

- high value

another day spent wanting you

and many more to go.

- the road to happiness

i was on your side
when people labeled you
as untrustworthy.

in the end,
i found myself
as one to not trust either

because i was proved
so wrong.

- i made a mistake, and now i can't trust myself with decisions like these.

you fell out of love with me
but it really does suck
because here i still am
in the same room
we both were in
when we first
laid eyes on each other.

- not over you

there's just something about you
because
i'm still okay
with reconnecting
even after all that you did.

- *toxic hearts*

after enjoying watching
the new rom-com,
i was told,
you're such a hopeless romantic.

yes,
that's definitely me.

- perfect description

though i have lack of experience,
i tend to center my attention on things
i never even had in the first place.

this applies to love and affection.

- *naive*

it's funny because

i didn't allow my brother
to annoy the heck out of me
with his constant chatter

and so i told him,
get out of my room.

i didn't allow my cousin
to tell me funny jokes
with his witty humor

and so i told him,
stop that, dude.

i didn't allow my best friend
to tell me what i should do
with her potential advice

and so i told her,
this is what i'm still going to do.

but what i did allow
was you
to send me mixed signals
and play around with me
until it was too damn late

and i fell in love with you.

- a fucked up logic

all this pain
you put me through
yet it's still you
i want to be close to.

- forgive and forget

i still try to cover up what you've done, the mess you made, and the
hearts you chose to break (including mine). i've always liked to think
that it was all a bad dream, or perhaps even just a prank. and this
i know is embarrassing, because it hurt way too fucking much for it
to be fake.

- contradictions

we spend so much time
trying to chase after
the ones who left

yet
we tend to be less attentive to
the ones who actually stay.

why do we do this?

it's so damn wrong.

- what heartbreaks leave us with

heartbreak follows me
like a lone shadow.

one person
to the next.

- everyone seems to be the same

it's kind of concerning how
after all this time,

you're still stuck
in my mind.

because at this point,
i'm not sure if it's still a crush
or whatnot.

- persistence

despite us parting ways,
i still want to show up
at your front door

with your favorite
coffee and pastry you'd order at brunch
in hand.

with your favorite
movie we'd always watch on friday nights
in hand.

with your favorite
vinyl record we'd listen and dance to
in hand.

and i'm hoping that if i do,
it'd be like the scenes from the movies
where we'll run into each other's arms
without hesitating even a bit
and you'll welcome me back into your home.

- *if our love was strong all along*

i just want to tell you how i genuinely feel. if there weren't so many circumstances or obstacles in the damn fucking way, we probably would've been confessing so much, and i would've gotten the answers i've been seeking for; like if you feel the same way about me too.

luck is just not on our side. *but will it ever be?*

- *maybe just maybe*

dear me:

please just stop
falling for the one
you absolutely cannot have.

- let go

the idea of us
is the sole reason why
i still believe
in *love.*

- visions

i wonder how late night drives would feel
if you were on the passenger seat for once
holding his hand while the other steers the wheel
and knowing this wouldn't just last for months.

- 3 a.m.

longing for and picturing love
is a satisfying notion.

that is until
it never comes true.

- *false belief*

i knew you weren't
the one for me
the second you hurt me
and i found myself in
the darkest room of my life.

so,
why didn't i stop there?

- *endless tolerance*

there's not one time
where i never returned
back to your profile.

- *i still love you*

a part of me feels guilty and sinful for still wondering about you, even if it was just once for three seconds. because you did me wrong in the worst way possible, yet i still left a little fraction of me to wonder about you to the point where i still care about you.

and no, this isn't satisfying or pleasurable, it's painful.

what can i do to wash this fucking pain away?

- wtf am i doing?

just because one person
fractured your heart,

doesn't mean
others will.

right?

- hoping for the best

i hope when i meet him
the same energy will be exchanged

that way all this waiting i've invested
won't go to waste.

- reciprocation

i loved you,

but did you
love me?

it sure didn't
seem like it.

so why did i
even do it?

- *a wasted love*

all the promises you would make
were the reasons why i chose to stay

until you left me
and i realized
they didn't mean shit at all

so i really could've
left earlier
to avoid
all this mess.

- *a promise is a fucking lie.*

sometimes,
i think to myself
why i even write about you
because in reality,
you really don't deserve it
after all the shit you pulled.

- silly me

and here you got me
writing about you
again.

- routine

| 3 |

grief

the feeling you have when remembering the pain and suffering you experienced when you gave the person you thought would be your all, your all.

it wasn't the way you left, the way you had me stressed, the way you easily progressed, or the way you made me depressed.

it's the simple fact that you left.

- the root cause

i have a bittersweet feeling
towards romantic comedies.

they're what keeps my excitement
and lightheartedness alive.

but,
they blind the possible dangers
and impossible certainties

of a *happy ending.*

- pros and cons

things happen for a reason
is a phrase i always hear.

weird thing is that
i never knew the reason
as to why you broke my heart.

- it doesn't add up

you blamed it on *bad timing,*
but the only thing to blame
is the other girl you were deciding.

- too many at once

i'm not lying
if i said it was gallons of tears i cried
and felt like dying
when you dumped me on the roadside.

- *true sorrow*

i couldn't see your true colors,
so i thought you'd brighten my world.

but you painted it black and white.

i couldn't see your true intentions,
so i thought you'd love me unconditionally.

but now you're forever out of sight.

- i only saw the good in you

what happened to us?

we used to be the duo
everyone admired.

- astray

the worst part about
losing your soulmate is that
not only did you lose
the one you loved

but you also lost
the only one
who ever understood you.

your whole damn
best friend.

- scarred for life

falling in love:

the most perilous risk
you could ever take.

- *do it as you please.*

you were the last person i had ever expected an abrupt ending with. there was so much more i wish we had in store. i guess this is what happens when we promised and loved too much.

- unforeseen

you sure had a way
to entice me into thinking
love is an ecstatic feeling.

but ever since you left,
i only find it
traumatic and displeasing.

- *bruises*

how crazy is it
that the one you loved
became the one you hate?

- *reversed*

the person i loved
sadly slipped away.

the person i loved
sadly chose to betray.

the person i loved
sadly caused me dismay.

the person i loved
sadly went their separate way.

the person i loved
sadly *didn't stay.*

- *the person i loved*

it may seem like us falling apart wasn't such a big deal, but when you look deeply into it, you'll start to grieve.

unpursued air flights to the east coast, absences from reservations at the brand new eatery, and empty promises we made that we'd stay together to this day.

- grief

the best things
you could've done
to make this work
was just *try and stay.*

- but you didn't.

the first love

became

the first heartbreak.

- *firsts*

you're not really a criminal

but how many heartbreaks
are you responsible for?

- *guilty*

and here you are
doing what we did
with another.

- replaced

so, how are you doing now that i'm not around? do you finally feel relieved that there's no wasted love wandering on the ground?

- *liberation*

he was all
i ever wanted.

too bad
it didn't happen.

- wasn't meant to be

loving him
meant
hating me.

- trying to measure up

i really wanted us to work out.

and it's funny how
i gave max effort
for us to work

yet
i've never contributed
that same energy
to my own dreams.

- self-sacrificing

call me simpleminded;

because,
that's the title
i deserve

after time spent
loving you.

- the fool

i just miss the times
i was infatuated with you
prior to knowing
your *true colors.*

- *aftermath*

it's like we didn't even matter;

you went ahead
and fucked with somebody new

not even one month in.

- *the second we split*

i know it hurts to lose something.

but oh god, it killed me when i had to lose you.

- what felt like death

we were almost there;

almost
in love.

but we were just

not quite there.

- almost.

the saddest part about being broken
by somebody else is that

an innocent and genuine person
will eventually come and truly love you

but,
you'll be afraid and doubt them
in ways they don't deserve.

so,
who is really to blame here?

- *repercussions*

had we not made the promises we did from the start,
we wouldn't have been in this tough spot.

- things we said but never meant

don't break a poet's heart;

they may write about you.

- moral of the story

i wasn't one to love
yet i spent a chance
to try it with you.

but,
you only taught me that
in the end,
it's not worth doing.

- lost cause

when we talked, i told you all about myself. very specifically on what i liked and what i disliked. i told you my favorite kind of coffee that i drink every morning seven days a week. having that conversation made me laugh because you weren't fond of coffee like that yourself. but it actually became interesting to know because we were getting to know each other so much more this way and the connection clicked. i remember you even made fun of me and joked around saying the coffee explains my short height, hence the start of a new nickname you have given me. but now you're gone and we haven't spoken for about a year. and everyday when i drink the same coffee i told you about, my mind traces back to you and our conversations that day. when we were happy and when everything was going quite well.

- small talks, big memories

one mistake
can mess up
and put an end to
one big thing.

just like what happened

to *you and me.*

- heartaches and mistakes

the most ridiculous reason
for insomnia
is the ongoing thought
of you.

- dreary eyes, beliefs in lies

you had a kindhearted soul,
which is probably why
i fell in love with you.

but,
this all went the other way
when you became stone cold

and so the love burned down
like a wildfire.

we just couldn't coexist.

- departed

here lies
what could've been.

- our love's grave

2 is a perfect way
to describe myself
in your eyes.

i was the *2nd* girl
you would choose
when the first one
left you.

you loved me at a *2*
out of ten
when i loved you
a hundred percent.

you'd travel *2* miles max
to meet me at the cafe
when i snuck out my house
just to see you across the bay.

you thought we'd last *2* years
when i believed
we'd last way more
than we could ever achieve.

and i guess i'm the gullible one
because here we are now,
broken and done.

we lasted only 2 months.

- 2

how does it feel
when the one you abandoned
feels empty and ashamed

while you
are living life
wild and free?

oh,
you probably
can't even answer this,
since you'll never
be thinking about

this trivial but
crucial question.

- leaving what meant nothing

sometimes when i think about us again,
i only focus on the times
we were clearly into each other.

this helps to wash away
our ugly ending and
even fantasize
what we could've been
up to this day.

- short-term memory

in all honesty, there's actually one person from my past whom i shared this romantic fling with and still wish it lasted.

he was my first dream boy. he made the room light up every time he walked through the door. he was the first boy i've ever had intense and mature feelings for at such a young age. because of him, i was introduced to the *hopeless romantic* side of love.

but just like the other heartbreaks, we never lasted, let alone were even close to lasting. even though he broke my heart and betrayed me in some fucked up ways, i still fantasize over what we could've been had everything gone great. and the most pathetic part is that this whole thing happened years ago, yet i can't seem to get over the thought of him. the thought of us.

- a story i never told

what could we have done
to have those endings
as seen in the movies?

i've always wanted to know
the answer to that question.

- what could it be?

it's sad as shit
because it's like
i was already dying
with all i've already dealt with in life

and you,
the one i thought would save me,
turned out to be
the person who took
my last breath.

- *tragedy*

wow, you really did mess me up.

- i'm embarrassed

so,
are we lovers

or did we just
pretend to be?

- *make-believe*

did you really love me,
or was that just something you would say
in order to make me stay?

- because it sure didn't seem like it

you were certainly the transition of a sunny summer day to a stormy winter night.

during our first few months of talking, you introduced me to feelings i have never felt before. you know, the usual butterflies in the stomach, constant excitement from receiving phone notifications, and beautiful thoughts of you appearing inside my head. i was almost sure you were the one for me and that we were in the midst of progress.

but one day, you left me crying and confused. i don't know what went wrong, but i do know that i became lost in the darkness and fog. i sat there for a damn week waiting for you to respond to me. a few days before that, i had just confessed my true feelings for you, which i thought you clearly reciprocated.

you had told me, *i want this too.* but i'm pretty sure you went off to your friends telling them all this news and celebrated in vegas like it was your 21st birthday, which just meant nothing at all to you.

and so a week later, you told me the truth.

it was another girl worth leaving me for at no better timing.

and i played the fucking fool.

- ghosted idiots

when i look at it,
i didn't do anything to hurt you.

all i ever did
was love and care for you,
especially at your worst.

so,
my actions shouldn't have
lit a flame for you to
treat me like bullshit,
nor turn around
and deceive me.

now tell me
why you really did it.

tell me why you really paid me
with bad and undeserving karma.

- *confessions*

i wish that when you told me,
i'll do everything to fix what i broke
and make things right this time,
i knew it was a pretty lie.

that way,
i wouldn't have been broken
twice in a row.

- second chances = second heartbreak

how you know if someone truly loved you when they said it:

despite you parting ways, they would do anything and everything to gain you back.

and they would also never move on to someone new within the span of a year or so. or even never at all.

- silence can be a sign.

who knew
that concealing
a love

would be
so damn difficult?

- secrets untold

at the end of the day,
i've realized that
i've caught durable feelings for you
at such a wrong time,

because you don't even want me
the way i want you.

- bad timing

it's so sad
when you realize
that a love can't compare
to the one you had
with the one who badly hurt you.

- *nothing compares*

i feel sorry for the people i choose to shut out sometimes. i know
everyone is different and not everyone is the same. sometimes,
there's someone who just wants to give you happiness, prove
your doubts wrong, and wash away the pain. but i always think i
just gave too much trust to the previous person to the point where
nothing else remains. so at this point, i don't know what to do or say.

- *i'm sorry*

i know you think
you leaving
didn't upset
the fuck out of me

because i kept displaying
this *okay* feeling

but in truth,
i only did it
to upset you,

but the tables
have only turned.

- *the tables have turned*

i didn't want
a bouquet of flowers
nor expensive jewelry.

i simply wanted
to be cared for
even if you decided
to leave me.

but you still left
so recklessly.

- my feelings weren't taken into account

the demons in my head
are the reasons why
my feelings for you
were never said.

- constant overthinking

she loves him,
and sad thing is
he can never know

for the reasons
it's best to leave it
just as it is.

- what's best to leave out the mess

our conversations
become fresh ideas for you to talk with her
while they remain a memory for me.

our inside jokes
become a way to establish humor with her
while they remain a memory for me.

our favorite records
become the music you sing along with her
while they remain a memory for me.

our promises
become the permanent bond between you two
while they remain *just a memory for me.*

- advantages

it kills me to know
that i still wonder about you
and what we could've been
had things gone the right direction.

while you on the other hand,
have happily moved on.

new job,
new car,
new house,
new school,
new girl,

and a whole new life,
with me no longer in it.

- one fresh start, one broken heart

i couldn't make you stay,

and sad thing is
i never knew what could've.

- *still puzzled to this day*

it's like you become even more hung up on the person when they leave
you rather than when you're happily with them and know you'll be
forever. because, you're not living in fear knowing that they will
someday break your heart and everything you both have will go
to waste. sadly, when the opposite happens and it's the end for both
of you, you live in the realm of constant heartbreak and loss. and this
i know results in grieving and clinging onto a love that you thought
would last.

- saying goodbye to happily ever after

i love getting drunk.

it helps me sort of forget
the pain you once put me through.

- temporary relief

i'm bleeding to death,
and you're only showing me
that you give no ounce
of care.

- *wtf am i to you?*

last night, i struggled to put this puzzle together. and even though none of the pieces were missing and they were all sitting out in front of me, i somehow managed to be so clueless and couldn't even place any in the correct spots.

and honey, this very much reminded me of something in particular. like when i've witnessed the red flags and faults you brought out into this relationship, yet nothing still seems to add up. i just don't get why the fuck you made this chaotic shit happen, when it was already perfectly put together at the start.

- solving the mystery

sadness took a toll on me
just like loving you has.

- *stress*

i keep on trying to tell myself that i'm fine. i keep on forcing myself to do anything and everything that'll make me feel at least in the slightest okay.

but my mind, body, and soul just can't fucking take it anymore.

why did you have to leave me when i needed you most? why did you promise to stay with me throughout the span of this whole lifetime when instead, your words became a ghost? why did you bring up the idea of us traveling the world together, yet you went with your new girl to the east coast? why did you tell me you loved me, when you know damn well you weren't even that close?

- exhaustion

what could i have possibly done
for you to stay?

or was i just not enough?

- questions left unanswered

never mind the way i felt about you.

never mind the way i said i loved you.

never mind the way i miss you.

never mind all this lovesick bullshit.

- never mind

you know, i tried to understand why you did what you did. why you left when i stayed. why you quickly moved on when it took me 57 days. i wished things never had to result in never talking ever again, even if it would take a year or so.

but now i know what went down. you were a broken soul that i tried and tried to fix. i created the image in my head of you being a sweet angel who would never dare to hurt me.

however, the one i thought i could save became the one who left me stranded at the burning bridge ready to fall down and drown.

- the trust has died

| 4 |

ecstasy

the feeling you have when remembering the happiness and golden moments you once had with someone – feeling as if they will never go anywhere but stay here with you.

i should erase you
completely from
the depths of my mind.

but here you are
living in it
while i write this poetry.

- trips down memory lane

i didn't need therapy

because i simply had you.

- *my medicine*

were you a sweet dream
or a nightmare?

can't seem to figure that one out.

- uncertain

i don't think
anyone has ever
made me feel

both happy
and *sad*
coincidentally.

- *your power*

i've never been more excited
to go to bed
and dream of us
once again.

- sweet illusions

we became lovers
in my own *fantasy land;*

where i visit
when asleep.

- REM

he's very poetic.

he makes me want to
write words
and verses
about him
and the way
he makes me feel

literally all the time.

- my muse

since i cannot text you or literally tell you all these things, i am going to let poetry do the job.

- feelings i want to show and words i want to say

i liked it best
when you were here.

- *golden moments*

writing about you
has become,
well,
a daily routine.

imagine
what thinking about you
may be.

- habits

all these faces in the world
yet i'm still searching for yours.

- you're the one i want

some will say that *i'm only in love with the idea of you*, but they don't know the truth.

i'm in love with your personality. the way you make me laugh when i have a bad day.

i'm in love with your courage. the way you assure me with bold words when i'm in doubt.

i'm in love with your strength. the way you make sure nothing gets in the way to defeat us.

truth is, *i'm in love with you.*

- the truth

even when you're only on the screen
and not physically here,
you still manage to
increase my heartbeat.

how?
i don't even know.

- a one-sided relationship

why do you do this?

you keep me up
wanting you more

and more.

you're honestly
the most addicting
drug.

- *addictions*

though it seems i'm sad most of the time,
there sure is a party up inside my mind.

why?

because it's constantly clouded
with memories of us,
the sounds of our conversations,

and the way it reacted
when you said
i love you.

- the opposite

i still think about you
like the way you had these plans in the future.

i still think about you
like the way you adored my sense of humor.

i still think about you
like the way you said everyday i only get cuter.

i still think about you
like the way you set me as the wallpaper on your computer.

the point is
i still do,
but i don't know about you.

- one-sided thoughts

i got lost in the cold
looking for somewhere to settle.

then you gave me your arms to hold
and told me, *stay, darling, you'd never meddle.*

and i knew then that i was home.

- *home*

am i crazy
for thinking that
you'd feel the same way
if i spoke up?

i hope not.

- for when i finally have the courage

i don't know how to specify the exact thing going on in my head lately.

all i know is that i've been thinking about you and picturing us being together in ways that i envision inside my mind. and if i'm being quite honest, you're always in my brain before i go to sleep, when i sleep, when i wake, and when i stay up late.

is this just a crush, or am i really *in love?*

- i really wish you knew how i felt; i'm just scared of rejection

i didn't know if it was your touch, smile, personality, or eyes that made me fall into this track you have me stuck in.

but,
i'm honestly enjoying the ride.

- *ecstasy*

everyone has left me
broken and wounded
in the past.

will you be the one
to make me forget

or just remember?

- please be different.

why does
the thought of someone

feel like
the best substitute

for therapy?

- the cure

sometimes i wish
it was all a big nightmare
and that you and i
are still lying beside each other,

and i'll wake up
with your hand in mine.

- *still here in reality*

you really hold a
special title because

you made me the happiest,
yet you also made me the
most miserable.

- you had the best of both worlds.

if only
everything
you told me
were true,

we probably
would've been
hand in hand
walking on
the beach sand.

- how it should've went

the butterflies i get
when i see you
should be an obvious sign
that i'm in love with you.

but to be honest,
they can be quite annoying
because they stop me
from confidently talking to you.

- i don't know if it's a good thing or a bad thing.

before i met you,
i wasn't looking for anything.

however,
you had my mind changed
when we met.

because now,
i'm looking for you.

who am i kidding,
i'm looking
for *us*.

- love at first sight

i've never met someone
as heartwarming as you.

how could i be
so damn lucky?

- words i wish i can say someday, sometime soon.

| 5 |

wisdom

realizing what you truly need to have and do; your true obligations (making yourself a better person solely for you – and not for anybody else).

lovers
can be
enemies,
too.

- *something i wish i knew*

the ones who stay
become
the ones who leave.

remember this.

- what will happen later

i would so willingly
take the chance
to erase the day we met

if i ever could.

- *maybe it'd help*

i sat in a cafe yesterday with a close cousin, catching up and having small talk. somehow, you were brought up in the conversation, as we began to discuss old relationships that have fallen off. and it's been a while ever since i even thought about our break.

while i was recalling and describing how we fell apart, i started to ache. a whole part of me relived the pain and misery you had put me through before. but i finally remembered the exact reasons why someone i was as close as to you was no longer in my life.

then reality struck back to the present, and i was feeling great as ever. and i have every reason to feel thankful for the reasons we fell off and broke.

- *weights off my shoulders*

i hate to admit it but,
those who are afraid of love
because of commitment
are pretty damn intelligent.

i wish i had that mindset
before my heart got broken.

- a wise choice

you may have never noticed,

but the saddest part
about the phrase,
it didn't work out

is that when they leave
and they're forever gone,
it's much too late.

and at that point
it makes no more sense
to try to *stay and wait.*

so it's best to just
move on with life
and go your separate way

even if it means
doing so completely
without them.

- a love that will never rekindle

the day after we fell off, i know you probably thought i didn't give a fuck about you anymore. because i didn't bother reaching out to you again or pulling the *i'm so sorry about last night, let's put this past us and never speak of it again* card.

but in truth, i was bothered and wounded as hell. of course i was. i hated to watch someone i loved and literally talked with 24/7 fade away from my life. i couldn't even sleep the nights after and went to school and work with baggy ass eyes.

eventually, i found that it was what i had to do. it was a hard decision, but i couldn't keep holding onto someone who didn't love me the same and only kept me around to have someone who spent their time and effort caring for them like a mother's child.

and so i took all the love and care i gave to you and turned them into self-love and self-care.

- the best decision

i've grown tired of finding pathetic excuses to make up for
your mistakes.

there's no more *buts* i'll say to my friends.

and there's no more *running back to you* to make amends.

- *no more*

i spent so much time
hanging onto the idea
of sharing love with someone else,

that i forgot how to
love myself.

- i should start caring for myself more

it's okay to want a love
who won't break you
even in the slightest bit.

you'd be so damn lucky
if you ever achieved that.

but,
it's not okay
to want a love
if it means breaking
your own self

for the other person.

- respect both sides

truly accepting that love
won't always have a happy ending
is the best thing you can do for yourself.

you'll then save yourself
the years of trauma, misery, and heartache
its bad ending can trigger you.

- *self-care of being aware*

i'm trying to be
the bigger person
and let you go.

- maturity

this love thing is really not worth it;

save yourself.

- *wisdom*

the unpleasant part about loving too much, especially on one specific person, is that you become hard on yourself without even knowing it. you'll spend so much time trying to fix yourself to be better just for them, just to be noticed by them. and when you change yourself to fit a *perfect image* you have created in your head, you won't even know if they themselves would be attentive to it.

and so you spend and waste a whole lot of time loving someone who doesn't even love you the same way, when in reality, you should've just been loving yourself. even just a little bit of selfishness doesn't kill you; it's a damn necessity.

- unhealthy tendencies

honey, if you're hopelessly romantic, make sure you don't go all out and give them your all.

some people don't deserve it.

- playing it safe

she knows better than to choose
the people that she'll just lose

and to accept no excuse
for those to only put her to use.

- *i know better*

we can try and perceive
love in a way we witness
in the movies;

but we know damn well
it won't always be like this.

- *the way it really is*

yes, i'm a hopeless romantic.

but, i'm not stupid
to the point where
i'll let you use that
as leeway to strip down
my worth.

- *it won't happen*

i've always lied and said
dating isn't for me.

in fact,
i only say that
to prevent

the eventual
heartbreak
that comes with it

once you get
too comfortable
with the person.

- taking precaution

these sad songs don't even make me feel sad anymore.

instead, they are just now a reminder of why our fall and break was needed in order for me to wake up and realize all the mistakes you repeated and how you were such a good damn liar who was only conceited.

so, i'm turning up the volume to its highest.

- reminders

to the one who left me:

thank you so much for giving me the opportunity to know that not all love is sunshine and rainbows. although you left me broken, bruised, crying, and confused, there's nothing more i can say but just thank you. thank you for the heads up, my love.

- at least you taught me something

for now,
i'll only be
working on
and looking out for
myself.

- my mind, body, and soul: under construction

and here i thought needing
a special someone
was needed for me
to feel complete and succeed.

- *i was so wrong*

and now that i know that you'll never return, i think i finally decided to take the healthier path.

i never found happiness chasing after you, but maybe i can finally be at peace and make myself a better person by choosing me.

- choosing myself

you are on the path to realizations
and finding your true obligations.

- the first step: self-love and self-care

it's like
cutting our ties
made storms disappear
and all that was left
were the clearest skies.

- *cotton candy*

after we parted ways,
i decided to work on the ways
i distribute my trust.

though it took more than a few days,
i am happy to say
i am way more than tough.

- no one will fool me anymore

this is not a promise, but a *try* from now on:

i will try my absolute fucking best to get you out of my head. i know the thoughts of you, us, and love are constantly sticking to my brain, but i think at this point, it's enough.

if i now have the power of noticing what is too much or unhealthy, i think i can manage letting you go, right? even if letting you go means just for a while or just taking a break. i would take this chance instead of never trying and persistently hoping.

and so i'm going to try and do what's best for me. not what's best to keep the thoughts, memories, and fantasies of you and us alive. i need to fix myself. i need to break those unrealistic thoughts and habits. i know the person i thought you were or the people we could've been will never come back, let alone yourself.

so, *goodbye for now, my love.*

- signing off

poems and cover art by
francesca joanna

other books by francesca joanna:
teenage melancholy

and more to come.

about the author

francesca joanna is an artist, writer, and college student
born and raised in northern california.

she started reading poetry during her early high school
years. after falling in love with poetry, she began to
express herself through her first collection, which is
her very own *teenage melancholy*. after self-publishing
teenage melancholy, she began writing her second poetry
book, *the mishaps of a hopeless romantic*, out of heart as well.
francesca aspires to release more poetry collections in
the future, sharing her works of art, stories, and messages
with the world.

another of francesca's passions includes music. during her leisure time, she enjoys singing covers of popular songs and writing her own original songs. she frequently posts her music on her social media platforms to share this other love of hers with others.

follow the author:

instagram: francescaxjoanna
youtube: francesca joanna
soundcloud: francesca joanna